TECHNICAL
Virgin

HOW
FAR
IS
TOO
FAR?

TECHNICAL
Virgin
HOW FAR IS TOO FAR?

HAYLEY DIMARCO

Revell
Grand Rapids, Michigan

Hungry Planet

© 2006 by Hungry Planet

Published by Fleming H. Revell
a division of Baker Publishing Group
P.O. Box 6287, Grand Rapids, MI 49516-6287
www.revellbooks.com

Printed in the United States of America

Library of Congress Cataloging-in-Publication Data
DiMarco, Hayley.
    Technical virgin : how far is too far? / Hayley DiMarco.
        p.   cm.
    ISBN 10: 0-8007-3085-2 (pbk.)
    ISBN 978-0-8007-3085-7 (pbk.)
        1. Sex—Religious aspects—Christianity. 2. Sexual absti-
nence—Religious aspects—Christianity. 3. Teenage girls—Sexual
behavior. 4. Sex differences. 5. Sex differences—Religious aspects—Christianity. I. Title.
    BT708.D545 2006
    241'.66—dc22   2006001112

Published in association with Yates & Yates, LLP, Literary Agents, Orange, California.

Contents

Introduction: Two Roads to Sexual Destruction 11
Are you on one of them?

1 **Technical Virgin 19**
Or as I like to say, "Abstinence—everyone is doing it."
Why is a commitment to abstinence just as dangerous to
your health as no commitment at all?

2 **Innocent Flirting or Sexual Foreplay? 37**
Are you giving a guy mixed messages when you flirt?
Setting the stage for a full-on sexual encounter? How far is
too far in the world of "just playing around"?

3 **Friends with Benefits: And Other Female Fantasies 51**
Control! You want it and you think you've got it, but is
that really the case? Or is there something else at work in
your female fantasy?

4 **Female Porn and You 75**
Chick flicks and romance novels—how far do you take
your romantic fantasies?

5 **Guys Want Sex 85**
Guys will lie to you to get what they want, and what
they want is sex. What game are you playing? Is your
marketing campaign getting you what you want?

6 **Losing Your Emotional Virginity**   93

Sure, you might be a technical virgin, but have you lost your emotional virginity? How much of your heart have you given away?

7 **Sexual Activity Leads to Depression**   99

Did you know that if you are depressed, it might just be because of a guy? How can relationships lead to depression?

8 **Way Beyond Technical**   113

If you've messed up and done more than you wanted, don't despair. There is hope if you've gone beyond technical to all the way.

9 **So How Far Is Too Far?**   129

This is the end but also the beginning. Decide today how far is too far and stick to your guns.

Your Spiritual Entourage   139
Notes   155

65% of non-virgins
said their parents
think they are
still virgins.[1]

Introduction

Two Roads to Sexual Destruction

Guys are hot, and something inside of you glows whenever you think about them. You love the way they look, the way they smell, the way they talk. They are dreamy. And a certain kind of sensation runs through your body when you touch them or kiss them. You feel alive like you've never felt alive before. It's magical, and you want more. I understand—believe me, I understand. Fooling around, making out, and sexual encounters can all be amazing—even addictive! But how far is too far?

How far have you gone? Have you tested the waters and decided that they are good? Do you believe that abstaining from sex is God's will for your life, so you do everything but? *Technical Virgin* is for all of us who crave male attention but just don't know where to draw the line. We want more, we really do, but the questions are how much more and when? Can you feel like you've kept the faith if you are a technical virgin? I mean, that's the criteria, right—virginity till marriage? **But what really constitutes virginity?** I'm assuming for the purposes of this book that you really want to please God and that your sex life isn't out of control; it's just something you want to know more about from God's perspective. This isn't a book that will condemn you for what you've done. But it will hold you to a higher standard, a godly standard. And it will ask you to **start thinking long and hard about your sexual experimentation and how far is too far.**

The way I see it, two roads can lead you to sexual destruction, and I want to talk about both of them. You may find that, depending on your personality, one might describe you better than the other. As I go through the different aspects of your sexuality, keep in mind that your goals should be pleasing God and protecting your reputation.

I want you to create for yourself an image you can be proud of. If you read my book *Sexy Girls: How Hot Is Too Hot?* then you already know all about creating the perfect image. Everyone has an image, just like a Hollywood starlet has an image. Everyone creates a PR campaign, whether they know it or not, and all the people they come in contact with decide who they are and how to treat them based on that image. When it comes to your sexuality, you need to understand that what you are doing with guys has a huge impact on your reputation and your image. So getting back to the two roads that can taint your image and lead you to sexual destruction, have a look and see if either one fits your life right now.

If you aren't honest about where you've been, then it will be really hard to figure out where you are going.

ROMANCE VS. RECREATION

The way I see it, there are **two kinds of girls.** First there are **the ones who crave romantic attention.** They want their life to be the perfect chick flick. They look for guys who will shower them with gifts and attention. Maybe that's you. You love romance, and you are looking for Mr. Perfect to travel down the rosy path of love with you. The romantic girl can run into trouble, though, when she lets romance blur her vision and take her somewhere sexually that she never thought she would go.

The other kind of girl is the one who doesn't really look for the romantic moment; **she's just in it for rec-reation. Sex has become a pastime,** something fun to do with a guy or a group. It might sound weird to the romantics, but some girls just love the physical stuff and don't need all the romance that comes before it. This kind of girl is more likely to hook up on a class trip with a guy she has had her eye on but hasn't dated. These are the ones who like adventure, intrigue, and risk in their sex lives.

Both of these girls—the romantic and the recreational sexy girls—end up creating a sexy PR campaign for themselves that everyone around them will see. Because they both end up in the same place—getting in too deep sexually.

Both the romantic and the recreational sexy girl have wants and needs. And both of them see guys as a way to meet them, but they do it in different ways. In *Technical Virgin* I'll talk about both ways and help you to understand your wants and needs better so that you can manage your PR campaign to the world the way you want to manage it—and the way God wants you to manage it.

So before we get started, **let's do a little personal assessment.** It's always best to be honest with yourself when exploring God's purpose for your life. If you aren't honest about where you've been, then it will be really hard to figure out where you are going. **So ask yourself this: how far is too far?** You have drawn some kind of line in the sand. Where is that line for you? Write it down here:

_____

Then the big question is, have you gone over that line, either accidentally or intentionally?

Yes   No

Do you consider yourself more like the romantic or more like the recreational sexy girl?

_____

What I hope you get out of this book is a better understanding of yourself and your limits. I want you to form opinions of your own based on what you know about God and his law. He has expectations of you, and you can fulfill them once you better understand what they are. So before we get started, let's do a little talking to God. Let's all admit to him that we need to know more about him and that we want control over our sex lives.

Dear Papa God,

I do have sexual thoughts about guys. I want to be loved and touched. I just don't know how far is too far. But I am willing to learn. I want to please you, and I want to remain pure as you ask me to be pure. Please help me to see where I have slipped up and to get back on track. I want to please you, and I know that I can do that with your help. I promise to consider everything in this book, including the hard parts, and to study your Word along with it. I want to be holy as you are holy.

Amen.

Great! Now that we are all on the same page, let's take a look at God's Word and the world's ways when it comes to sex and you.

chapter 1

TECHNICAL
Virgin
Or

Abstinence—
Everyone Is Doing It

Have you signed an abstinence pledge? Are you devoted to abstaining from sex until marriage? If so, bravo. Abstinence before marriage is not only God's plan for sex, it's also the only way to avoid pregnancy and STDs 100 percent of the time—or is it? Researchers at Yale and Columbia University found that teens pledging virginity until marriage are just as likely as their peers to contract or discover they have an STD. Huh? How can that be? If they're abstinent, what is going on here?

Well, here's the rub (no pun intended). The truth is that those of you who pledge abstinence are more likely to have oral and anal sex than other teens who haven't made that pledge. Shocking? Or not so shocking to you? Guess that depends on your sex life, doesn't it?

There is an epidemic going on today that has to be addressed. Lots of adults are afraid to talk about it because it just seems too freaky, but I'm not one of them. **If we want to get real with ourselves and our God, we have to get real about our sex lives.** We can't keep on lying to ourselves as if that makes everything okay, 'cuz it doesn't.

Why are more and more "technical virgins" having more and more sexual encounters?

And what does God think about the "technical virgin" anyway? Is he all excited that you found a loophole? Is he happy that those of you who are sexually active without going all the way are having fun and doing what your bodies feel like doing just as long as you avoid the *f* word (fornication)? Oooh, don't get me started. Okay, do get me started! Let's take a logical look at sex and find out where we are going wrong and how to get back on track.

God forbids sexual immorality, or sexual intercourse, as most call it. Right? I think we all can agree on that. (If you're not sure about that, check out 1 Corinthians 6:18: "Flee immorality. Every other sin that a man commits is outside the body, but the immoral man sins against his own body." [NASB]) But then the lines get fuzzy. What is sexual intercourse anyway? Is outercourse just as bad, or is it a good "in the meantime" game we can all play till we get married? **If you are going to understand your sexiness, then you need to understand your position on sex. You need to decide right here and now what sex is and what it isn't, and what God allows and what he doesn't.** I am, of course, assuming that you are a Christian and that you care what God calls sin. You might not have had all the facts in the past, but since you have read this far in the book, it's too late to plead ignorance now. I can just hear your wheels already starting to spin. *Have I gone too far? What is too far? Will God forgive me? What will I do from here on out?* Those are all valid questions, and none of them are too hard for the power of Scripture to handle. See, if we are all believers here, then we all live by the same code, the same law,

31% of virgins

responded that they have been pressured by a guy to go farther.[2]

the same set of precepts that God set down thousands of years ago and that we can no longer afford to ignore. Check it out:

Technical Virgin: Someone who thinks she's still a virgin as long as she hasn't had intercourse. She thinks that anything up to that doesn't count against your virginity.

> Do you not know that the wicked *will not inherit the kingdom of God?* Do not be deceived: Neither *the sexually immoral* nor idolaters nor adulterers nor male prostitutes nor homosexual offenders . . . will inherit the kingdom of God.
>
> 1 Corinthians 6:9–10, emphasis added

We aren't just playing here. This is some serious stuff. If you don't really understand what constitutes sexual immorality, then you run the risk of missing out on your inheritance in the kingdom of God.

I did a little research on the topic, and here is some stuff I found out to help us understand what God defines as sexual immorality, a.k.a fornication. According to Webster's:

sexual immorality: being unchaste

chaste: innocent of unlawful intercourse

fornication: consensual sexual intercourse between two persons not married to each other

intercourse: physical sexual contact between individuals that involves the genitalia of at least one person

Satan is the master of subtlety. He loves to emphasize the subtle differences between things so that we get confused and start to sin but think we really aren't doing anything wrong. And he's confused us so well in the world of sex. Did you catch that last definition? Let's read it again: *intercourse: physical sexual contact between individuals that involves the genitalia of at least one person.* See, the enemy of God has done a masterful thing. He has convinced us that sexual intercourse, which you have pledged to avoid, is penetration, and penetration only. Things like mutual masturbation

and oral sex aren't included in the sin list God created for you. But guess what? *That's a lie.* If any genitalia are involved, then according to the dictionary, you are having intercourse. Surprised?

So let's just get things out into the open. When it comes to your purity, the sexual immorality that God detests includes the following:

penetration

oral sex

anal sex

mutual masturbation

petting parties

rainbow circles

hooking up

These are all part of sexual immorality. And if we want to get even more technical, then we have to look at verses like Ephesians 5:3: "But among you there must not be even a hint of sexual immorality, or of any kind of impurity, or of greed, because these are improper for God's holy people." God detests not only sexual immorality but also any hint of it, so in our definition we can include anything that might make people think that sex happened or is soon to happen—i.e., a hint of it. So let's see, what can we add to the list?

feeling him up

staying the night

him feeling you up

making out in public (everyone assumes you are having sex if you are so intimate with each other)

dry sex (a.k.a dry humping)

freaking (on the dance floor)

Anything that might give a passerby a hint of sexual immorality or, get this, give your body or his body a hint of sexual immorality is a sin. **Remember, guys are visual beings. They use their mind's eye to fantasize about all kinds of things about you.** And so you know that once you start doing something sexual like dry humping, they are going straight to the real deal in their minds. They are getting a real first-rate hint at sexual immorality.

I'm not going to tell you where to draw the line with the guys in your life. I'm not even going to say there is a line, but there is a Spirit. And that Spirit says, "Don't even hint about sex. I won't stand for it." So you have to decide what is hinting and what isn't. After all, you're old enough to make up your own mind, and you're old enough to suffer the consequences of your actions, whatever they may be. But I hope that after reading this and thinking it over, you will have some kind of "come to Jesus meeting" where you really start to think about how relaxed you have let your idea of sex become.

Here's what we said in *Dateable*, and I think it really helps to think about your time with your guy like this: Pretend there is a cameraman with you, shooting all your moves. Then at the end of the night your entire family is getting together to look at your slide show. "Here I am unbuttoning my top. Here we are rubbing on each other. Here we are swapping saliva." All while Granny and your mom look on in surprise. What would you be comfortable showing the entire fam? If you aren't comfortable doing show-and-tell later that night, then you probably shouldn't be doing it.

As believers we live by a higher standard than the rest of the world. We believe that our God gave us nothing but truth inside the pages of the Bible, and we trust that if we obey his law, it will go well for us. He will shower us with love, mercy, and grace. We trust that if we are obedient even in the hard stuff, he will honor us. It's like his Word says:

If you *fully obey the* LORD *your God and carefully follow all his commands I give you today, the* LORD *your God will set you high above all the nations* on earth. *All these blessings will come upon you* and accompany you if you obey the LORD your God: You will be blessed in the city and blessed in the country. The fruit of your womb will be blessed, and the crops of your land and the young of your livestock—the calves of your herds and the lambs of your flocks. Your basket and your kneading trough will be blessed. *You will be blessed when you come in and blessed when you go out.* The LORD will grant that the enemies who rise up against you will be defeated before you. They will come at you from one direction but flee from you in seven.

Deuteronomy 28:1–7, emphasis added

God blesses those who obey him. Even though it might seem hard right now, obedience to his Word is priceless. Decide right now if you will serve him or the enemy. Will you be obedient to his call to purity, or will you give in to your urges and the promptings of the world to satisfy your flesh and the flesh of boys? "It is God's will that you should be sanctified: that you should avoid sexual immorality" (1 Thessalonians 4:3). Will you be obedient to his will? If so, then tell him. Sign your life away today.

Father, I desire to be obedient in my sexual life. Today I turn from all hints of sexual immorality and turn toward your Word. Cleanse me from my past mistakes and help me to remain strong in the future. I am sorry I have strayed. Thank you for your forgiveness.

Signed,

_____

Fooling Around Ages You

If you think the hookup, the casual sexual encounter, or being friends with benefits saves your heart from heartache, think again. You are lying to yourself to get what you want. You want to fill the void. You want to stop feeling lonely and start feeling loved, but just like the midnight run to the fridge for a big slice of chocolate cake, it only fills the void for a few minutes, and then it's stomachache or heartache city. You don't protect your heart by allowing guys to use you sexually. The hookup is just a way for guys to get what they want—sex—without any strings attached. It's a way to turn you into a piece of meat that will be chewed up and spit back out. And you want the real kicker? It ages you. That's right. You want to look old before your time? Get sexually active. Each encounter you have gives you one more sign of wear and tear. Just like a used car, your value goes down with every mile you add to your sexometer. If you want to stay cuter longer, then cut back on the bad habit of sexual immorality. It will not only save your soul but save your appearance as well.

SEX STARVED

You might think, "That's all well and good, and I get that sex is sin and God doesn't want us to do it outside of marriage, but you don't understand. That's impossible. I have desires. I have urges. And who can go without satisfying them? I mean, it's impossible." And to that I say, I totally understand.

It's hard to resist. It's easy to give in. The feeling makes it easy. Guys make it easy. Your heart makes it easy. I can tell you from experience that it was the easiest for me to give in when I didn't have a good understanding of God's Word.

In high school I always knew that sex was wrong. I got that. But I didn't know how far was too far. I didn't know what else, if anything, was bad. And so I experimented. I let things go farther than I wanted. I didn't go all the way, but I fooled around pretty good. And each time it got easier. With each encounter I found that I could go farther and farther. And although something inside of me was gnawing at me, making me think, "This just isn't right," I didn't have the strength to stop it—until I learned the truth.

When **I got into God's Word** and found out what he really meant about my sexual life, I was in a very intimate relationship. I was out of high school and free to live the life I wanted. So I went for it. I fooled around. I was still sure sex wasn't for me, but I felt free to spend the night with my boyfriend every night all the same.

When a girl at church finally sat me down and got real with me, my life suddenly changed. She was the first person to put it to me straight. She laid out what fornication was and what sex was for. She didn't fear that I might leave the church or get mad at her; she just wanted me to be completely aware of God's Word so I could make a more educated and holy decision about my sex life. And it worked. The light went on,

and I got it. It was like night and day. I suddenly got it. I told my boyfriend all about it, but what do you know, he wasn't so excited. In fact, he left me. Disappeared, really. Never returned another phone call. Couldn't be found anywhere. He was just gone. Years later he said he just couldn't take all my "Jesus crap"—meaning no more fooling around. But that was the best thing that could have happened to me. At that point I got onto the right road. I found it much easier to commit to God's law and to stay true to it, even in the hard times. In fact, the hard times got easier and easier because I just knew that sex play was off-limits. Period. The end.

So don't think that I don't understand your situation, 'cuz I do. And don't think that I'm trying to make it sound easier than it is, 'cuz I know it isn't easy. But trust me, when you fully commit to God's Word and believe it to be true, you get stronger. The pull of sexual fulfillment suddenly doesn't seem as strong.

God's Word is truly powerful, just like it says. "For the word of God is living and active and sharper than any two-edged sword, and piercing as far as the division of soul and spirit, of both joints and marrow, and able to judge the thoughts and intentions of the heart" (Hebrews 4:12 NASB). It isn't some weak formula for having a better life; it is power. It is ultimate truth, and it is life changing. So don't worry about how you're going to stop or how you're going to control yourself. You just are. Trust me. God and his Word are going to help you. What I want to give you in the following pages is more ammo—more ways to cool down and take back control of your life. I want to make you aware of things you are doing that might be leading you into danger. Once you start to understand where your boundaries are, you will gain strength to stay pure.

That boyfriend who left me because I chose abstinence over him called me a few years later in agony. His life was falling apart, and he knew I had something that was bigger than any earthly relationship could provide. He wanted to know more about God, and that day he believed and his whole life changed. Since I'm not a big advocate for missionary dating, I pointed him in the direction of a church and some men who could help him on his new journey. Never underestimate the power of doing the right thing.

chapter 2

INNOCENT
Flirting
or
SEXUAL
Foreplay?

Now that we've talked a bit about the recreational side of sexuality, let's touch on some romantic moments. The girl with a hankering for romance might find that a little innocent flirting is just laying the foundation for sexual foreplay. **What might seem like just a sweet little encounter could actually be giving the guy a mixed message.** And in the end it could lead you to more sexual intimacy than you had imagined. Just playing around can get your motors running without you even realizing it, and suddenly you've left romantic mode and moved into sexy girl mode. Innocent flirting, or sex games, those things you do that aren't really sex but can quickly lead to sex, that's what I'm talking about. I mean, how romantic to be involved in a major tickle fight, to fall to the floor laughing, him on top of you . . . your eyes meet, and suddenly your lips collide. Pure romance, right? That's why I'm going to call all this kind of play sex games. Check them out.

THE BIG RUB DOWN

It's so wonderful when your guy gives you a massage, isn't it? You've been stressed all day, and the touching and rubbing just make you feel so relieved. He's really an amazing guy to give so much without getting anything in return. Or is he? I mean, he might be a great guy, but there is also more to it than just a kind gesture. For the average guy, touching you is a sexual thing. He feels your curves, he smells your skin, and he's thinking about what's underneath your clothes. **It is rarely a casual thing for any guy to massage a girl**—to him it's a sure sign she likes him. Because of the major testosterone that runs through the body of any normal, red-blooded guy, **he is going to be having some sexual thoughts of the girl he's rubbing down,** so he thinks it's the same for you. Don't be so naïve as to think it's purely platonic. When the guy you aren't interested in starts rubbing your back and you don't make him stop because it feels so darn good, **beware! 'Cuz he's dreaming for more than just a back rub.** And when it's a guy you're into, you can be sure he's thinking of taking it farther. Back rubs are really great foreplay. They relax you and get him ready for more.

If you talk to your guy friend about this and he's all denying it, **just ask him how many massages he gives to his 83-year-old grandmother** and see if that doesn't gross him out. Why? Because it's a sexual thing. I mean, you don't see a bunch of guys sitting around rubbing each other's shoulders at lunchtime, do you? That would just be weird. Why? Because it's a sexual thing. You getting it now? If you want to maintain your obedience to God's Word and not give a hint of sexual immorality, then stay away from back rubs. It's just a mixed message to the guy and a first step down a slippery slope. Save a guy's heart and don't lead him down a path that you aren't ready to take.

A guy never
has tickle fights
with his
buddies,
cuz it's a sexual thing.

TICKLE FIGHT

Ah, the tickle fight. You giggle; he tickles you more. You squirm; he grabs ahold of you. Harmless, nonsexual fun. Right? Or is there more to this as well? Just like the back rub, the tickle fight can get all your juices flowing. **Your blood gets pumping. Your hormones start raging.** And you can see the ending coming: He tickles you. You laugh, squirm, scream, and giggle. You fall down. He lands on top of you. You suddenly both realize how much you like each other as you gaze into each other's eyes . . . and *bam*! Your lips meet, and it's pure kissing bliss. The start of the perfect relationship.

But what's going through his head at the same time? He also imagines an ending: He tickles. You both laugh and look at each other longingly. You fall into each other's arms, kiss passionately, and spend the next hour having sex.

Hard to believe, I know, but it's true. That's how he's thinking. And if you talk to a guy who says, "No way, we aren't all thinking about sex when we have tickle fights," then ask him the same thing as for the back rub: **how many of his buddies does he have tickle fights with?** I bet he says none. Hmm, now why is that? **Because it's a sexual thing.**

The tickle fight is another dangerous sex game to play if you want to be sex free, because it's just asking for more. And at the very least, it's just leading the guy on to thinking there might be something more. So be careful.

NAP TIME

It's just so cozy. It's a lazy Saturday. Your parents are out. You're watching an old movie together, and then it hits you. You're both tired, it's so comfortable being together, so why not take a nap? I mean, it's harmless, right? So you cuddle up in the best position ever, the spoon. In this close position you can feel his heart beat. He's warm all over. He's breathing on your neck. Your mouth starts to water. **Let me just say that it doesn't take a psychic to figure out where this is going.** It's foreplay. Yes, it is. And besides, talk about a "hint" of sexual immorality. When the family walks in, they can think all kinds of things. I mean, this is a sexual position. Let's just forget about the hint on this one. This goes way beyond a hint because it puts you both horizontal. It paves the way perfectly for sexual intimacy.

If you are taking naps with guys, then you're feeding your raging hormones and his and making it almost impossible not to go farther. I don't want to sound like a total prude here, but just think about it. Don't lie down together and you can save yourself from falling into the sexual temptation that God's Word warns us against.

It's not enough to agree that sex is wrong; you have to agree that guys are visual creatures and that you have a huge responsibility in protecting them from your body. When you let them massage you or lay skin on skin with you but never intend to go further, you aren't being abstinent—you are being a tease. A tease destroys the spiritual mind of the guy because she leads him to stumble in this thought life.

SKIN ON SKIN

As you continue to slide down the slippery slope of sexual intimacy, the next thing you are likely to hear from your guy is how much he just loves to feel skin on skin. It's not about sex, just the warm feeling of flesh against flesh. But don't kid yourself: if this isn't foreplay, then I don't know what is. And foreplay is for the express purpose of getting our bodies ready for intercourse. **It's impossible for a guy to lie next to you skin on skin and not imagine having sex with you.** It's just where his mind goes.

Now, before we go anywhere else on this slippery slope, let me explain one very important spiritual fact. Jesus makes it clear that our sins aren't just in our actions but start in our minds. In fact, he's so clear on this that he says in Matthew 5:28 that **just thinking about having sex with someone is counted against you just as if you actually had sex** with that person. Read it for yourself: "You have heard that it was said, 'Do not commit adultery.' But I tell you that anyone who looks at a woman lustfully has already committed adultery with her in his heart" (Matthew 5:27–28). You can't get around this. This isn't some ancient, out-of-date concept that we gave up on years ago. It's the Word of God written down for all to see and all to be judged by. If you are going to let your guy daydream about having sex with you, then you've essentially led him down the path of disobedience. And God is very clear about sexual sin.

It is God's will that you should be sanctified: that you should avoid sexual immorality.

1 Thessalonians 4:3

I have written you in my letter not to associate
with sexually immoral people.

1 Corinthians 5:9

The acts of the sinful nature are obvious: sexual
immorality, impurity and debauchery.

Galatians 5:19

We can't continue to lie to ourselves and say that
these kinds of sex games are okay in God's eyes and
we aren't doing anything wrong. That might have been
the case before you knew the truth, but once the truth
is revealed, you have no more excuses. Sex outside of
marriage isn't a game to play. It's a dangerous toy that in
the end leads you to heartache, disease, and unwanted
babies.

THE PROVERBIAL SLIPPERY SLOPE

All of the things listed here are part of that romantic journey down the slippery slope of sexuality. The path is obvious, and the slide happens over and over again. If you're on it, you're not the first to go down it, and you won't be the last. Yours isn't some romantic journey that is unlike any other; it's run-of-the-mill, happening all over the world, and terribly, terribly unhealthy for your soul. The progression is usually the same: it starts out with the "innocent" back rub, then goes to the tickle fight, to napping, to napping without shirt or pants (I mean, it's just like being in your swimsuit), to laying together skin on skin, to heavy petting, to sexual intimacy in any number of ways. All this stuff we've been talking about is all made to lead to one ultimate thing—sex. Intercourse, oral sex, masturbation, whatever kind of sex you choose, it's all made to lead there. So the next time you think that what you are doing with your guy is just innocent flirting, tell yourself the truth and get real. It's all about the sex.

I know that you probably don't want to disobey God. I know you want to have a great relationship with him and to be holy and righteous. I know that you love him and talk to him and pray to him and that you didn't mean to fall into temptation. And that's why I've said all this. The more you realize the truth about your own sexuality, the more you can control yourself and be obedient to his Word. This is no longer a game; it has ramifications both spiritually and physically, not to mention emotionally. (I'll talk more about that in "Sexual Activity Leads to Depression," page 99.) Be safe. Be real. And stop the game. Sex isn't made for that.

Really Good Sex

Sex isn't made for people who aren't married, but sex is perfectly designed for one man and one woman in marriage. Seems to go without saying, but I thought I should add it in here anyway.

chapter 3

FRIENDS WITH
Benefits
And Other Female Fantasies

Sometimes us girls can live in a real fantasy world. We get so wrapped up in our emotions that we think guys have the exact same emotions as we do. And then we start to project all these things onto them—things we think they are feeling or thinking and things we feel or think. But the truth is that guys think and feel totally differently than us girls. They have completely different brains when it comes to sex. They see things differently, do things differently, and mean things differently. Unfortunately, as girls we can get so caught up in the moment and our own rush of emotions that we forget how different guys really are.

On the whole, a teenage guy's focus isn't love and romance; it's sex and getting sexual. Sounds harsh, but just ask your dad or any man who won't lie to you and he'll tell you that guys are sexual beings. And that taints every interaction that they have with girls. We can't forget that when we are trying to figure out how to relate to them. For example, girls are more romantic, or as some would say, delusional. We think that everything has a deeper meaning or can get us to a deeper meaning. We hope against hope for true love. Even when we know we won't get it, we still arrange our lives so that maybe, just maybe, with the right combination

On the whole,
a teenage guy's
focus isn't love and
romance; it's sex
and getting
sexual.

of circumstances, our Prince Charming will come our way.

We also lie to ourselves about our emotions.

A lot of us want to be really strong and stop acting all girly, so we try to play it tough, as if we don't want love and romance. We substitute other stuff, like the just plain physical, in an attempt to feel more in control. And it's true, it feels like a position of weakness to need romance and love. It's a vulnerable set of desires we have, and guys can totally rip our hearts out when they know that. So a lot of girls, and maybe you're one of them, have decided to play the game more like guys—emotionless. And you think that will give you more control. You come up with ideas like friends with benefits or recreational sex games in order to feel more detached from the female ache for true love you have inside. The truth is, though, this attempt to give yourself more control and more freedom from your feminine side might just be backfiring on you. If you've decided to detach yourself from the romantic world and get down to just enjoying the physical or using it to eventually get what you want, then look out, because you could be headed for disaster.

FRIENDS WITH BENEFITS

A friend with benefits is a guy you hook up with just for the physical but never commit to as a girlfriend. It seems effortless, a great alternative to the lonelies. You are friends. You like each other's company. Neither one of you has a significant other. So why not hook up, have some fun, and call it a day? Seems almost healthy. I mean, how much more detached and unemotional could you be? With this revolutionary arrangement, there isn't any jealousy or hurt feelings. You don't feel trapped in a relationship that isn't "all that." You have a friend and you have the benefits. Bingo! What a great combo. You dive into a "no strings attached" relationship that fills your need to "get a little attention" but does it without any of the risk of commitment.

Sounds like power, doesn't it? You're in control of your own destiny. You don't need a guy to make you happy, just a buddy who is willing to meet some of your physical needs. But is the power really in your hands? Have you really set yourself up for success? Let's take a closer look and see.

Whether you realize it or not, **girls have something that guys crave.** Guys are continually thinking about us and how to get more of us. We are in demand. So what happens when you make a casual agreement with a guy to be just friends with benefits? Does your power increase? Do you suddenly have more of what he's looking for, or have you just given up the part of you that was the most valuable to him? The truth is that if guys are so hot for our bods and craving intimate attention, that's where our power lies. And it's not in giving ourselves away casually but in using what we have, our bodies, as bargaining chips. In the old days, a guy knew that if he wanted sex or sex play from a girl, he had to marry her. That was her bargaining chip. That's how she got her Prince

Being a "**friend with benefits**" is like Starbucks deciding to give their coffee away instead of charging and then wondering why they are going broke.

Charming. But as girls started to crave some kind of false power, they started to give away the very bargaining chip that could get them what they ultimately wanted.

It might seem like a small thing to share with a friend— a few kisses, some make-out sessions. But it's really giving up what you have going for you. **It's like Starbucks deciding to give their coffee away instead of charging and then wondering why they are going broke.** Now, don't get all confused and think I'm saying we should sell our bodies, 'cuz I'm not. What I'm saying is that one of your most valuable assets in getting a guy to commit to you is your body and your loving, and when you give it away indiscriminately to your FWB, you lose some of your value. You cheapen yourself.

But maybe you are saying, "Who cares? I want some loving, and I'm getting it. Maybe it's him who is losing his value." To that I say, okay, let's say you want the loving so much that you aren't willing to wait for your own man. Consider this. Fooling around with a guy creates all kinds of feelings. Those things you were trying to be in control of, they all start growing. And it could be that it's only one sided, with one of you feeling more than the other. What do you think that does to the relationship? Gets kinda weird. When it comes to fooling around, emotions run high, and some changes are bound to happen between the two of you. So what happens when one of you finds the person of your dreams? What happens to your FWB then? Do you bag the friendship? Do you just stop that crazy sex stuff you were doing? How do you walk away from what you already started? The truth is that most of the time the new relationship changes things. Relationships drift

Friends with Benefits might seem like a simple, uncomplicated relationship. But the truth is that it's one of the most complicated ones you can create.

apart. Feelings get hurt. Tempers can even flare. It's like they say: you're playing with fire.

Essentially what you are doing when you create an FWB bond with someone is saying that God's way ain't your way. You've decided that the sexual life that God considers so sacred isn't really a big deal at all. And you are spitting in his face. You are telling God and everyone who knows about your arrangement that your physical needs are of ultimate importance—more important than your faith, and more important than God's law. FWB might seem like a simple, uncomplicated relationship, but the truth is that it's one of the most complicated ones you can create. You give away a very special part of yourself. You lead the mind of the guy down all kinds of paths. And worst of all, you cheapen the sexual relationship. You make sex and fooling around, all that intimate stuff, disposable. In other words, you practice cheapness. You are creating for yourself and your friend a world where your body and your sensuality is cheap. Heck, it's so cheap, it's free. And then when it comes to the marriage you may someday have, look out, because you will have set a precedent for yourself when it comes to sex stuff, and that precedent is that it's no big deal. But God says it's a huge deal. It's the thing you only share with one man, your husband. It's meant to be a special thing between the two of you, not a casual thing you've shared with a bunch of others.

Face it, **FWB is not in your best interest.** It establishes in your mind and the minds of those around you that your sexuality is cheap and that your needs take precedence over God and his law. And it opens you up for a world of heartache when the situation changes. If you think you have more control over your love life by having a friend with benefits, you are lying to yourself. **You've only cheapened your value in the eyes of your friend** and the world.

STOLEN LOVE

Another fantasy we can live under is the fantasy of stolen love. It's simple, and it goes like this: **when a guy is dating another girl and he dumps her to be with you, you feel totally special.** You think, "Wow, I have something she doesn't." And so starts the lies. The truth of the matter is that you aren't more special. You're just more special *for now*. Because as we said in *Dateable*, if I'll do it for you, I'll do it to you. If a guy will break up with someone to be with you, his character shows that he will break up with you to be with someone else. So don't buy the lie that you are more special because he left her to be with you. You are just the girl in his sights right now. It doesn't bode well for his character to be a guy who loves 'em and leaves 'em. So stop the fantasy. He isn't better for you than for her; he's just feeling restless and ready to move on.

When you lie to yourself about a guy's character, you really lose control. You start to let his flaws taint your vision, and you lie to yourself even more. If you want to be in control of your love life, don't date someone who just broke up with a girl to date you. Make him prove himself by taking some time with no girlfriend before he starts up with you. Then you'll be in control. Then you'll be making smart decisions, not emotional ones.

If I'll do it **for** you,
I'll do it **to** you.

IF I LOVE HIM I SHOULD

"If you loved me you would," he said, and so you did. I mean, you love him, so I guess that means you will. After all, a guy can't live without sex, can he? He has needs, and sex is a big one. So you think to yourself, "Maybe if I give him what he wants, he'll give me what I want. Our bond will grow stronger. We will understand and love each other more." But that's where girls get it wrong. Sex does not equal love in the eyes of a guy. That's a girls' fantasy gone wild. Sex just means he's finally getting what he wants for now—and that's sex, not love. For a guy the two really don't have anything to do with each other. His mind is so focused on the physical that it's truly all he's thinking about. This can go on for a while, and you might think it's making you closer, more intimate, but the truth is, it's just making you less important and more used up.

I've heard guys say that they could never marry their current girlfriend because they were having sex with her. They want their wife to be more pure than that. Seems crazy, I know, but it's true: guys want sex with whoever will give it to them, but once they get it, the excitement is gone. The chase has ended, and the adventure is over. Soon they will feel the need to move on to the next target, leaving you in the dust. I know, I know, not *your* boyfriend. He loves you. He even tells you that. But let's not forget that guys lie to get what they want, and what they want is sex. It's not that they are all dogs; they just want to give you what you want, love, so you'll give them what they want, sex. And so he says, "I love you." But he also loves his car and his Xbox and the Green Bay Packers. So don't take the love words you get from physical stuff too seriously. When sex is involved, guys will say anything to keep it coming until they're ready to move on.

It is a lie that if you loved him you would. The truth is, if he loved you he wouldn't. When a guy holds you in high esteem, he doesn't want to take your sex from you; he wants to protect you and your honor. Don't become a statistic by believing the lie that if you loved him you would. It's just another female fantasy that guys play on to get what they want.

ORAL SEX IS THE SAME AS KISSING

This fantasy is more than likely one for the recreational sexy girl rather than the romantic. The romantic might be thinking, "What in the world?" But hang on, it's true, some of you girls think oral sex is the same as kissing. It's harmless, innocent fun that never hurt anyone. All over the world, girls and guys are giving in to their desires for sexual satisfaction by casually participating in oral sex. If you're a girl who had no clue about this, I'm sorry to burst your bubble, but it has to be addressed because something sinister is at work here. This casual acceptance of oral sex as something as mundane as kissing is tearing up the fabric of the female mind. So for you who have joined in on rainbow circles or casual oral sex for fun or money, let's have a serious look at what you've gotten yourself into.

In the summer of 2000 *Twist* magazine did an online survey of 10,000 girls, over half (5,700) of whom were under 14. Amazingly, 24 percent of the girls who said they were virgins responded that they engaged in oral sex.[4]

More often than not, oral sex is all about the guy. **It's all about pleasing him and does nothing for the girl other than make her a tool that he can use for his sexual satisfaction.** If you think that performing oral sex on him will make him like you more, think again. The truth is, it only cheapens you in his eyes. You become nothing more than a prostitute, offering services to any man who asks. Don't believe me? Then let's just look at the definition of *prostitute*.

prostitute: a woman who engages in promiscuous sexual intercourse especially for money

Notice that they add "especially for money," meaning it isn't just girls who do it for money but also girls who do it for nothing.

A fall 1999 survey of 15-to-19-year-olds by *Seventeen* magazine found that 49 percent of respondents considered oral sex to be "not as big a deal as sexual intercourse." Further, 40 percent of respondents said it did not count as "sex."[5]

Having casual oral sex is making yourself a prostitute, plain and simple. And last time I checked, being a prostitute wasn't such a good thing. In fact, it's the lowest of lows. See what God has to say about the matter:

> For a prostitute is a deep pit. . . . Like a bandit she lies in
> wait, and multiplies the unfaithful among men.
>
> Proverbs 23:27–28

Notice God blames the woman for her evil ways, not the man. He just warns the man about her. If you are allowing a guy to use you for sexual satisfaction, then **you are leading him down a path of destruction, and God is blaming you.** As girls we have to stand up for what is right. We have to take a stand against impurity and not let guys convince us to lead them into sin. As I've already stated, to lead someone into sin is a dangerous thing, and you will be held responsible for it.

As if all this isn't bad enough, casual oral sex can also cheapen you in your own eyes. **The mental and emotional ramifications of oral sex are worse than you think** (see "Sexual Activity Leads to Depression," page 99). Something inside of us naturally knows that giving oral sex to men in this kind of way is degrading. It makes us less a girl in control and more a girl being used. Nothing good comes out of it for the relationship. Again, you just become a set of lips that he can use for his sexual fantasy. And the sad truth of the matter is that it is you who carries the risk of STDs. Yes, you can get STDs from oral sex. This isn't just innocent fun. It could be a sentence to anything from HPV to herpes, hepatitis B, and gonorrhea.

When girls have oral sex with guys, they decrease their own value and teach guys that girls are just playthings, not to be taken seriously. The guy gets all that feels good out of the relationship,

Just because you are avoiding penetration doesn't mean you are avoiding disease. HPV *(human papillomavirus)* is a cancer responsible for 99.7 percent of cervical cancer cases and the deaths of nearly 5,000 women each year.[6] If ingested orally through oral sex, it can be responsible for both head and neck cancer and oral warts.[7]

and the girl gets both figuratively and physically put down onto her knees like a common slave.

The truth of the matter is that all of us girls have the capacity to lie to ourselves about guys and what they are doing with or "for" us. We can cover up all the stupidity by calling it a girl's prerogative to choose. But the truth is that these girl fantasies we create are really destructive. They are slowly devaluing girls and teaching guys that we are just tools of the sexual trade, available for their casual sexual fantasies. **It doesn't build your power or prestige among guys.** It doesn't make them like you more. And it is acceptance of full-on sin in your life. The lies you tell yourself about your nontraditional relationship with guys are slowly killing the very core of who you are and making you nothing more than a sex toy for guys without character—not to mention what they are doing to your spirit. Consider God's Word before you decide that "my sexual fantasies are okay," "forgiveness is just around the corner," or "I'm covered by grace."

If we say that we have fellowship with Him and yet walk in the darkness, we lie and do not practice the truth.

1 John 1:6 NASB

The one who says, "I have come to know Him," and does not keep His commandments, is a liar, and the truth is not in him.

1 John 2:4 NASB

Sexual sin constitutes walking in darkness. It's a blatant statement that God's law isn't important to you, at least not as important as your sexual satisfaction. And according to his Word, if you think you know him but you purposefully choose to sin anyway, you are a liar and you don't know him. Ouch! Scary concept. Don't be one of the ones who think they know God but are really only faking it. Purposefully walking in sin—knowing it's wrong but doing it anyway—proves that you don't really know God at all. Now, we all occasionally slip up. That's normal. We confess, repent, and receive forgiveness. But don't lump the occasional slip-up in with a choice to live a life of sin. They are two different things, and God makes it clear how he feels about the second when he says:

> Many will say to Me on that day, "Lord, Lord, did we not prophesy in Your name, and in Your name cast out demons, and in Your name perform many miracles?" And then I will declare to them, "I never knew you; depart from Me, you who practice lawlessness."
>
> Matthew 7:22–23 NASB

Stop playing with fire. A life of lawlessness will be

much harder to live with than a life of abstinence, trust me. It is worth any degree of grief now to have God say to you when you meet face-to-face, "Well done, good and faithful servant." You have the power to control your mind and your body. With God's Word by your side, you can do anything—or not do anything, as the case may be. **The choice is yours. Be sure to choose wisely; it will affect the rest of your life.**

chapter 4

FEMALE PORN
and You

I think the best part about a relationship with a guy is the romance. Don't you? I mean, chick flicks aren't the most popular kind of movie for us girls for no reason. The dreamy guy who sweeps the girl off her feet with a bed covered with roses and love poetry from his heart . . . who doesn't love it? We all eat it up. And guys go along with us begrudgingly, but you don't see a bunch of guys going, "Hey, let's go see that new chick flick tonight. I'm really jonesing for some romance." It wouldn't happen. But chick flicks, romance novels, anything that makes us feel the rush of romance is all right with us girls.

There's something exhilarating about a beautiful romance unfolding before your eyes. It can even get your heart rate going. It's pure excitement. I can remember going to see a particular chick flick and at the end of it turning to my friend and saying to her after a deep exhale, "I need to go home and take a cold shower!" The guy totally had me going. I wanted some lovin'! It was then that it hit me: *Oh my gosh, I'm acting like a guy who just watched a porn movie.* **I was dreaming about some fictional character on the big screen.** My mouth was watering. I wanted what the leading lady had with him. I was starting to feel a little depressed because "I'll never find a guy like that—one who rescues me from the Russians and sweeps me away to a romantic cabin for a much-needed restful and dreamy weekend!"

Chick flicks and romance novels: female porn. They do the same things to us that porn does to guys, only they play on the part of love that we crave—not all the physical stuff but the romance. Being chased, wooed, showered with gifts. Looking longingly into each other's eyes. Long, slow kisses. Holding hands. Skating in Central Park. Wrestling in the grass. Tickle fights. All the things we dream of are put on-screen in the montage created by directors and producers who really get the female psyche. It's female porn.

You might say, "So what's wrong with that? What's wrong with watching romance on the big screen or reading about the perfect man in a romance novel? I mean, it's not sexual. So what's the big deal?" Think about it like this: when guys watch porn, they get this image in their minds of the perfect woman, one who is more than likely totally different than the average girl. And they start to expect sexual perfection. They dream of doing what they see on the screen, and it perverts their thoughts about real girls. How many of us look like or act like porn stars? So how is that any different from what we do with female porn? When we see or read about romance, **we begin to expect romantic perfection.** We start to hold guys to higher standards. We want them to be our knights in shining armor who rescue us from our mundane lives and mean parents. We expect pure perfection out of them, and we get disappointed when that's not what we get.

Female porn does the same thing to our minds that male porn does to a guy's: it deludes us by creating a fantasy person who isn't real and was never meant to be real. **When guys don't live up to our expectations of the perfect leading man, we complain.** Or when we don't have a leading man for ourselves, we get depressed. "Why can't I get a guy like that?" we whine. Female porn can be a dangerous thing for the female psyche, teaching us all kinds of lies about the relationship between guys and girls.

The truth is that the guys at your school have probably not mastered the role of leading man in a chick flick, and it's unfair to demand that they do. They have other things going on in their

Female porn does the same thing to our minds that male porn does to a guy's mind: it

deludes us

by creating a fantasy person who isn't real and was never meant to be real.

Danger Zone: Female Porn Impairs Judgment

You might love to go to chick flicks. You might even drag your boyfriend along or want to see him afterwards. But beware, because doing that can cloud your vision when your eyes move from the screen to your relationship. Watching a chick flick can leave you feeling a rush of excitement over seeing the perfect man and the perfect romance. It's just as sexual to us girls as seeing a woman naked is to a guy. Chick flicks can be like a drug that keeps us coming back for more. So beware, you are at your most vulnerable to slipping up sexually after watching a "good" chick flick. That's because when you leave the theater your guy can really look good. Your mind can trick you into believing that a sixteen-year-old male who doesn't have a job, still lives with his parents, and plays Xbox all day *really is like Matthew McConaughey.* You believe that he's the cause of your excitement. Don't lie to yourself; you are feeling hot and bothered because of the flick, not because your date's Mr. Perfect. And the flick was fantasy, pure and simple. So be careful next time you go to a chick flick—you might do something you regret.

lives. And I guarantee you that **if they seem to have mastered the romance stuff, then it's for one reason and one reason only: to get you into bed.** I know it sounds harsh, and I'll sound even more harsh in the next chapter, but guys for the most part have one thing in mind, and it ain't the perfect romantic weekend. Guys give romance to get sex, just like girls give sex to get romance. It's a mixed-up world, but it's the one we live in. And the key is to understand your own desires and needs, all the while understanding his needs and desires so you don't fall into the black hole of sexual sin. Sex isn't something we should play around with, so perhaps romance isn't something we should take lightly either, since it was created to lead directly to sexual stuff.

I'm not trying to be harsh here. I just want you to see that what you put in your mind determines what comes out in your life. And God's Word makes it clear that we are to maintain our purity. If that requires that we abstain from daydreaming about romance, then so be it. If chick flicks, romance novels, and your favorite love song make you think about how badly you want a guy, then maybe, just maybe, these things are distracting you from your real purposes in life. Maybe they are clouding your mind with desires and wants that aren't available to you yet (and even making you depressed). And what's worse, maybe they are setting you up for relationship disaster. I'm not saying these forms of entertainment are inherently evil; I just want you to think about what they do to your thought life. What kind of expectations do they create in you? What kind of daydreams do they generate? Romance isn't a toy for you to play with, a pastime for your idle pleasure, any more than sex is any of those things. Romance is foreplay. It's preparation for falling in love, marriage, and forever. So maybe you might want to think about not taking it so lightly.

Consider the fact that what comes out of us in actions first takes place in our minds. We first conceive it (or dream about it) and then do it. "But each one is tempted when he is carried away and enticed by his own lust. Then when lust has conceived, it gives birth to sin; and when sin is accomplished, it brings forth death" (James 1:14–15 NASB). Lust for us girls starts with romance. It starts with a dream, and it progresses from there. Romance just softens us up for what comes next—intimacy. So be clear about what you are playing with when you play with romance.

Like I said before, romance isn't an evil that must be avoided, but I think all of us girls should consider and be aware of its power so that we don't become addicted to romance and lose sight of our desire for holiness and purity. Romance can cloud your eyes and get you distracted from your commitments. It's that first step down the slippery slope that can end in sexual sin and leave us bruised and battered emotionally. Romance isn't something to take lightly. It is an amazing gift that has the power to envelop your heart and rock your world—just don't use it all up on your latest crush. And please, please don't let it cloud your thinking and lead you into sexual sin.

chapter 5

GUYS WANT
Sex

I've said it before and I'll say it again: guys want sex. You might think, "That is such a cliché. Not all guys are like that. They don't all go for the physical." But I've never found a man or a group of guys who would dispute me. Sure, a guy might tell you it's not true and they really have no sexual cravings at all, but he'd be lying to get what he wants—sex!

Now, this isn't some horrible thing. They aren't all jerks; they are just hormonal. It's natural. God made them that way. It's how we perpetuate the human species. But when you're not looking to grow humankind, you have to be careful with a guy's urges. You might be thinking, "Good, 'cuz I want sex too. It's fun." But before you dive into the deep end of the pool, let's talk about the ramifications of a guy's drive.

You might think you like the physical just as much as the guy, so he's not pulling anything over on you. Stop! Not true. A guy wants sex for the sex, period, the end. His urges want to be satisfied. But us girls are different. Sex isn't something we can have and then forget. God made us a little different. He made us more sensitive and vulnerable. He made us to bond through sex. We give up the inner parts of ourselves to a man. He enters us, and we become one with him. We feel a connection like no other when we have sex. Guys might say they feel a connection, but they don't feel it to the same degree we do. They feel it in the moment, but it doesn't linger with them the way it does with us. (BTW, it's that deep emotional bond that technical virgins are trying to avoid, fooling themselves into thinking that's the only part of purity that matters. Not true.)

In the United States more than 19 million STD infections occur annually. Half of them are contracted by youth ages 15 to 24.[8]

Girls make a mistake when they think that sex will keep a guy around. Because it bonds her to the guy, she thinks it bonds him to her. But that's not the case. A guy can much more easily move on to the next hottie. He can compartmentalize—put your memory into a box and forget it forever. And whether you want to accept it or not, us girls just aren't the same. When a guy gets sex, he gets what he wants: sex. When a girl gives sex, she gives it to get what she wants: intimacy, love, attachment. Trouble is, those don't always go along with sex or sex play.

If you still don't believe me, think about this. Who has more of a problem with pornography, guys or girls? I'm talking about the kind with naked people of the opposite sex, this time. Guys do, of course. Many, many of them are addicted to the stuff. They just love watching naked women. It's a craving for them. But very few girls get their kicks from looking at a bunch of naked guys prancing around. That's because we are more turned on by the romantic than by the physical. We might enjoy the physical, but it isn't our ultimate goal like it is for the guy.

So what happens when you give a guy what he wants (outside of marriage)? What happens in the relationship? He wins. He gets the goal of his game, which is sex. And just like when you play a game and win, you either want to start over and see if you can win again, or you want to go on to a new game. Trouble is, if that game was too easy to win, he isn't likely to want to keep at it too much longer because he prefers a challenge. And that explains why guys can move on so easily to the next girl. Sex achieved, game over, move on to the next game.

But maybe you've been dating a guy for a long time and having sex and he hasn't left. Let's talk about that scenario. If you are in high school, the relationship you are in right now statistically has little chance of lasting to marriage. That means you are going to break up. And what happens when you do?

What does your PR campaign look like to the rest of the world? How do you think other guys think of you now that you've been sexually active with your boyfriend for a long time? Do you think that makes you more appealing or more used up? Do you think a guy thinks highly of a girl who gave herself to a guy for so long? The truth is, it kind of makes your sex life a done deal. It's like that guy used you all up and didn't leave much for the next guy. And even if that doesn't bother you, let me tell you that the breakup will. Breaking up with someone you've been sexually intimate with might be the hardest thing you will ever do. You feel like you are losing half of yourself, and essentially you are. Healing from that can take a long, long time.

What if you aren't fooling around with a guy but you're just dating around? Lots of guys get to spend time with you. You don't go all the way. You play around, but that's it. What could be the risk in that? Well, getting back to the guy's goal, sex, it's not just a personal goal. Oftentimes it's a group thing—that is, they love to share their exploits with one another. It makes them feel special. It's how they get notoriety a lot of the time. So a guy might have gone out with you and then gone into the locker room the next day. All the guys are smiling at him because they know he went out with you and they know you date around a lot, so they are wondering how good you are. He can't handle the pressure, so he makes up some story about your animal nature, and *bam*! Your PR campaign has been written for you. You now have a reputation of a loose girl, and even if it isn't true, getting that rep to unstick will be like getting gum off the bottom of your shoe on a hot summer day.

See, when it comes to guys and sex, you have to be careful, because they can completely ruin your reputation if you allow them. And the way you allow them is by giving a hint of sexual im- morality. That is, by fooling around with a lot of guys, or dating one particular guy for a long time. The trouble with this last scenario is that you start to play house and act like you're married. Pretty soon people start to think of you like a married couple, and married couples have sex. So either way, you run the risk of ruining your reputation. Beware of how guys think and talk about sex. If you want to control your own image and what others think about you, then you have to know that guys want sex. Period. The end. They will do what they can to get it, and they don't often understand how to keep their mouths shut once they do get it. Guys who are getting sex can't be trusted. Just the fact that they will have sex before marriage shows a lack of character that doesn't bode well for how they will handle your reputation. So beware.

chapter 6

LOSING YOUR
Emotional
Virginity

If you're a romantic, then this chapter is for you. As girls we bond by talking. We get closer and closer the more we share our feelings and innermost thoughts. It's just how we are. And that is especially the case if you are a romantic. You want nothing more than for a guy to "get you." You want him to know everything about you and still love you. It's that age-old desire to be completely accepted for who you are. And how can you be accepted for who you are unless they know who you are? And how will they know you, I mean *really* know you, if you don't tell them all about yourself? So you talk and you talk and you share and you share. You have long phone conversations that make you feel like he's definitely the one because you can talk for hours. You spend eight-hour dates talking and sharing your deepest, darkest feelings. All these things feel like such a fantasyland. I mean, the perfect guy is the one who will listen to you, I mean really listen to you, and like it, right? But what if you're getting more than you bargained for in this arrangement?

First of all, let's get one thing clear: **guys are not like girls. They do not bond by talking.** They bond by shooting hoops, playing a video game, or watching the Super Bowl—none of which involves talking. For them, talking is a foreign concept, created by little foreigners called girls. They have learned that if they want a relationship out of us, they have to listen, and some have even learned that the more they listen, the more they can get out of us. Don't be naïve. They don't spend hours talking to you because you are interesting; **they spend hours listening to you because maybe, just maybe, it might lead to something more,** shall we say, something physical. A lot of girls scream in protest when I say stuff like this, but it's true. Ask any guy on the planet, and if he were to give you an honest answer, he would say that what he wants most out of a girlfriend or a date isn't deep, intimate sharing, romantic notes, or cozy dinners; what he wants is some sort of physical payoff. It's the way he's made. So for him the time he spends with you just talking is an investment in the future. That doesn't mean he's a scumbag; it just means he's a guy, and guys have different wants and needs.

Here's where the trouble comes in. When you share all your deep stuff with a guy, you run the risk of sharing with someone who won't always be there for you. In fact, he might one day break up with you, take all your deepest secrets with him, and start dating your enemy, the mean girl who totally has it out for you. Or he might just think it's fun to share your deepest, darkest secrets with the guys. It's a dangerous road to give too much of yourself away before it's safe. And when are you safe? Time helps the safe factor, but really no one's secrets are safe without the commitment of marriage. Because as we said in *Dateable*, if you're 14, 15, 16 years old, the statistics show that your relationship will not last. You will break up. And he will move on. So just be aware that when you give too much of yourself emotionally, you run risks. **You risk falling too hard for him, and you risk his spreading your goods around like cheap peanut butter.**

51% of teen
marriages end in
divorce
before the age of 24.[9]

Here's God's take on the topic:

The one who guards his mouth preserves his life; the one who opens wide his lips comes to ruin.

Proverbs 13:3 NASB

Above all else, guard your heart, for it is the wellspring of life.

Proverbs 4:23

Guard your heart by not letting too much out of your mouth. It's not just common sense; it's God-sense. Guys love a chase, and the more info you give him, the less he feels he has to chase. So be a bit more mysterious. Rest your mouth and let go of the need to be known intimately by someone you might not be with tomorrow.

chapter 7

SEXUAL ACTIVITY LEADS TO
Depression

Have you been feeling kinda depressed

lately? Really want a guy but no perfect guy is to be found? Or maybe you've found a guy but you aren't sure where you stand with him? Guys can rock your world. They can make you feel magical, and they can make you feel devastated. But did you know that they literally can make you depressed? That's right: "One study of 8,200 adolescents, ages 12–17, found that **those involved in romantic relationships had significantly higher levels of depression than those *not* involved in romantic relationships.**"[10]

Did you know that suicide is the third-leading cause of death for teenagers?[11] In fact, "one-third of the adolescent population has thought of killing themselves."[12] And the truth is that most of the depression that leads to these awful thoughts comes from relationships. Who would have thought it? But statistics are proving that **if you are in a romantic relationship, you are more likely to be depressed** than those who aren't in one. I always thought it was depressing *not* to have a guy, but the truth is, it's more depressing *to* have one. Go figure.

A full quarter (25.3%) of teenage girls who are sexually active report that they are depressed all, most, or a lot of the time.[13]

THE TRUTH ABOUT "SEXUAL HEALING"

It's like this. You might think that you'd feel so much better if you only had a guy and some good, good lovin'. You might think that the sexual stuff you are doing right now isn't the cause of any grief or depression but your hope. But let's take a closer look at that. Is sexual fun really the answer to your blues, or could it be the cause? According to Dr. Meg Meeker, a doctor who treats all kinds of sexually active young girls in her practice, "one of the major causes of depression is sex. . . . Teenage sexual activity routinely leads to emotional turmoil and psychological distress."[14]

Have you ever heard that before? Did you know it has been documented that becoming sexually active gets you depressed? It seems like it should be the opposite—"sexual healing," as the old song goes. But the truth is that something inside of you knows beyond a shadow of a doubt that giving yourself to a guy sexually is a compromise. A part of you that you might try to keep hidden still says, "He's using me" or "Things weren't meant to be like this." That might sound preposterous to you. You say you love the sex stuff. It makes you feel high. It's all you think about. But let me ask you: Do you get the blues? Do you sit around writing in your

journal and trying to figure out why you feel so down most of the time? Have you ever tied the two together?

I know that when I was in high school, even though I didn't go all the way, I still knew that what I was doing was wrong, and deep down I felt kinda yucky. I worried about my mom finding out. I felt bad that it was something I had to hide. I wondered if the guy would leave me and go fool around with the next girl. It just left too many open-ended questions.

THE BIG BREAKUP

As I've said time and again in my books, if you are in high school, **the relationship you are in right now, statistically speaking, will not last.** This is only a passing fancy. And everything you do with this guy right now will be branded in your mind long after the breakup. And the truth is, the farther you go sexually, the harder the breakup is going to be. **Sex complicates things.** It's such a giving of yourself. **Even if you aren't technically going all the way, it's still a major giving of your most intimate self.** But when the relationship doesn't progress into marriage, you break up. I mean, those are your options: either marry him or break up. And since most high school relationships nowadays don't end up in marriage, guess what? You're breaking up.

The truth is that breakups often lead to depression and even substance abuse. The pain becomes overwhelming. You feel like you can't go on, so you turn to something like alcohol to numb the pain. Ah, the joys of premarital sex. Don't be fooled. There are consequences for your "anything but" behavior. Even if you aren't going all the way, you are still going to face emotional consequences for how far you do go. So beware.

A teenage girl's anatomy is different than an adult woman's in ways that make her far more vulnerable to infection. For instance, the cells covering a teenage girl's cervix are physiologically different from the cells lining a 25- or 30-year-old woman's cervix, and they are therefore far more susceptible to infections.

STDs AND YOU

Being a technical virgin has not only emotional consequences but also physical ones. I'm sure you've heard it said a bazillion times in health class, but if you are fooling around—not even going all the way but doing everything but—you still run a high risk of getting STDs. I'm not going to beat a dead horse over this idea. You know it; you get it. Sex games are dangerous for your body. Gross stuff can and does happen.

But did you know that **STDs are also linked to depression?** Of course, it makes sense. Get a disgusting disease that hurts like heck, and you're gonna feel pretty down. So it goes like this: fool around and get STDs; get STDs and get depressed. Yay! How fun. Not! This is seriously gross and yucky stuff that even important people like doctors are trying to figure out. How do we help teens with STDs? You'd think it would just be ointments and stuff, but the truth is that it goes way beyond that. Now they are starting to screen you for depression if they find out you have STDs. The two go hand in hand.

SEX IS SO SPIRITUAL

A lot of people talk about sex as a spiritual experience, and it is. It was created by a spiritual God. But imagine (or maybe you are living it right now) what happens when you have given in to that "spiritual experience" and **now you are depressed not only emotionally but also spiritually.** Deep down you know you've disobeyed your God. You know that he was watching and that he isn't pleased, and so you distance yourself from him. At least you don't have to look him in the eyes and feel the embarrassment of failing. But the truth is, there is hope for you.

If you have done some stuff you aren't proud of and you know God detests, then don't turn away. Don't let the enemy own you by telling you to hide from God. **God can and will forgive you instantly. Spiritual depression doesn't have to last for you.** You have a relationship with God. You can go to him and get forgiveness. And not only is your spiritual depression going to lift, but this can be the first step toward lifting your emotional depression.

If you are sexually active you are much less likely to be happy and more likely to be depressed than girls who are not sexually active.

The truth is that **part of you might be grieving the loss of your virginity or of your commitment to stay pure.** And grieving is a process that takes time. Don't expect it to be over in a day. The stages of grief that you will go through will be denial, anger, bargaining, depression, and acceptance. But if you get stuck in denial, it will be impossible to get over the depression you might be feeling. Depression isn't something to take lightly. It's a "gift" from the enemy that has to be met head-on and fought. You have to realize that oftentimes it comes from doing something that is inconsistent with what you believe. And then you have to work through your feelings with God and his Word. I don't want this chapter to be a downer. If you are sexually active and depressed, you are already down enough. So let's see if we can't lift you up. God has ways of healing you that outdo everything the world can offer.

The first thing to do is to confess. You have to get real with God and tell him what you've done. Even though he already knows, confession is healing. "If we confess our sins, He is faithful and righteous to forgive us our sins and to cleanse us from all unrighteousness" (1 John 1:9 NASB). And you also need to confess it to another person. "Confess your sins to one another, and pray for one another so that you may be healed. The effective prayer of a righteous man can accomplish much" (James 5:16 NASB). Make sure this person is an adult who won't blab about your stuff. Try a youth pastor or close family friend who will listen and offer you God's forgiveness without condemnation or temptation to gossip. I did this exercise with a pastor at my church. I sat down with him and his wife and went through all the things I had done wrong sexually. It was the hardest thing I have ever done, but as I did it, I could feel the demons lifting. The enemy can't be in the light, and confession shines light on those dark places and heals you right up.

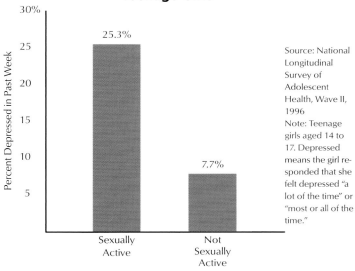

Depression and Sexual Activity: Teenage Girls

Percent Depressed in Past Week

30%

25.3%

25

20

15

10

7.7%

5

Sexually Active

Not Sexually Active

Source: National Longitudinal Survey of Adolescent Health, Wave II, 1996
Note: Teenage girls aged 14 to 17. Depressed means the girl responded that she felt depressed "a lot of the time" or "most or all of the time."

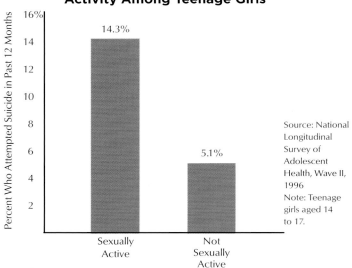

Attempted Suicide and Sexual Activity Among Teenage Girls

Percent Who Attempted Suicide in Past 12 Months

16%

14.3%

14

12

10

8

6

5.1%

4

2

Sexually Active

Not Sexually Active

Source: National Longitudinal Survey of Adolescent Health, Wave II, 1996
Note: Teenage girls aged 14 to 17.

The next step is repentance, which means STOP. Stop doing what you've been doing. Turn away. Walk away. Run away. Promise yourself and God that you won't do it ever again.

The depression we are trying to kick will disappear if you do these two things. Sure, the memories will always be with you, but you have to shut them off. Each time you start to remember one of your mess-ups, say "no," then stop the memory and replace it with something else. Like God's Word says, "Finally, brethren, whatever is true, whatever is honorable, whatever is right, whatever is pure, whatever is lovely, whatever is of good repute, if there is any excellence and if anything worthy of praise, dwell on these things. The things you have learned and received and heard and seen in me, practice these things, and the God of peace will be with you" (Philippians 4:8–9 NASB). Don't dwell on what you've already confessed. That just means you don't trust that God has forgiven you and you want to commit the sin all over again by just dwelling on it. Don't go there. Refuse to relive even emotionally what you've already been forgiven for.

Sex = depression. And having a guy isn't always the

answer to all your worries—in fact, he can be the cause of all your worries. Guarding your heart and your body is the best way to avoid depression. But if you've already gone too far, don't fear; God is near. You can have a clean slate and a clean mind. Don't let "everything but" sex or going all the way destroy who you were made to be. Don't let a guy have the chance to hurt you with his words or his body. The technical virgin isn't as happy as the girl committed to waiting for it all. Trust the statistics. Believe the doctors. Sex games lead to depression, but you have the power to save yourself by walking away now. Trust God to fill that empty hole you might fear will be left. He is ready and waiting.

Read over some of God's promises and reintroduce yourself to the truth. You are in good hands.

No temptation has overtaken you but such as is common to man; and God is faithful, who will not allow you to be tempted beyond what you are able, but with the temptation will provide the way of escape also, so that you will be able to endure it.

1 Corinthians 10:13 NASB

Therefore, there is now no condemnation for those who are in Christ Jesus.

Romans 8:1

In him we have redemption through his blood, the forgiveness of sins, in accordance with the riches of God's grace.

Ephesians 1:7

chapter 8

WAY BEYOND
Technical

"I lost my virginity." Is that you? Have you gone and done it? Gone all the way? It can be an awful feeling when you do. I mean, you didn't mean to. You hadn't planned to. It's just that things got going. Or the pressure was too much. Or you just changed your mind 'cuz it was so fun. But whatever the case, it happened. You did the irreversible, and you committed to something that changed your life forever. Having sex for the first time is a life-changing experience. For most of us it's painful both physically and emotionally. And it's never quite what you dreamed it would be when it happens outside of God's will. So what now? What do you do if you wish you'd never done it? Or if you now are starting to realize that it's not the lifestyle you want anymore? How do you change the past? Or better yet, how do you change the future?

There are a couple things to consider here. First of all, your spirit. **Your spirit is more than likely aching.** It's feeling the burden of fun gone wrong. If you've given any thought at all to God's Word, then you have to be feeling a tug right now that seems like it could tear the very fibers of your heart. You are probably asking yourself why. "Why with this guy?" "Why now?" "Why me?" And you are probably wondering, "How can God forgive me?" "How can I go on?" But take heart. You can and you will go on. Life will be a little rocky for a while as you work through your emotional issues—your feelings for the guy and your relationship with God. But the good news is that God is prepared. His Word makes way for exactly this kind of thing. In fact, his Son came to set you free from this mess you've made. If not for this, then why? (That's a rhetorical question. But a beautiful one.) If Christ came to set the captives free, then consider yourself about to be free.

It starts with a little thing called grace. According to the *Tyndale Bible Dictionary*, grace is "the dimension of divine activity that enables God to confront human indifference and rebellion with an inexhaustible capacity to forgive and to bless."[15] This essentially means that God's big enough to get the fact that you are prone to rebellion, and that he has the capacity and desire to forgive you for it and, yes, even bless you even though you've done what you've done. To put it bluntly, grace rocks! It's your do-over. It's getting off with a warning instead of a big, hairy speeding ticket. It's something we don't deserve but we get anyway. God wants to forgive you for all the stuff you've done, and he has the power to do so.

See, it's no secret to him that you're a mess. It's no secret to him that we're all messed up in one way or another. In fact, the apostle Paul writes in Romans 3:23 that we "all have sinned and fall short of the glory of God." So if you are beating yourself up over this, *don't.* It was expected. Humans bad. God good. And that's why he came up with the concept of grace. It's what salvation is all about. Not just salvation from hell and all that hot stuff, but salvation from each and every little and big mistake you've made. "For it is by grace you have been saved, through faith—and this not from yourselves, it is the gift of God" (Ephesians 2:8).

It's all about the blood—Christ's blood. He died in order to set you free from yourself. He died so that you could be forgiven and set free from the bondage of sin and all this messed-up stuff. It says so right in Ephesians 1:7: "In him we have redemption through his blood, the forgiveness of sins, in accordance with the riches of God's grace." So believe me when I say you are forgiven. As soon as you confess, you've taken a big leap toward forgiveness. But we'll get to that in a minute.

Before we do, let me just tell you the thirteen lucky words that changed my life forever. I had thoroughly messed up physically by doing more than I **knew** I should. I finally stopped, but I felt like I was forever branded. Forever bad. I felt like God could never really forgive me. I was haunted by my past and wondered how I could ever get free from it. I remember crying to a friend about my newfound faith. See, once I found out what God's Word had to say, I started to see things in my life that were way off. I had a hunch while I was doing them that they were wrong, but once I started reading the Bible, I knew for sure that I had completely lost it and traveled down the wrong road. I was in anguish. I felt so dirty, so unholy. So **not** grace material. But then someone gave me these thirteen words, and my life was forever changed. This changed everything. Here it is. Read this carefully, and maybe it will help you like it helped me:

Therefore, there is now no condemnation for those who are in Christ Jesus.

Romans 8:1

If you haven't read this before, or even if you have, you might want to check it over again. In fact, go back a bit. Start at Romans 7 and read through to this verse. Paul is talking just like me. He's talking about doing all the wrong things. Feeling almost compelled to do them. He sees the stupidity of his ways, and then he hits you with a whopper. The most unforgettable passage in Scripture, for me. No matter what you've done, no matter how bad, or how often, or for how long, there is NO CONDEMNATION for those **who are in Christ**. That's grace, baby! That's amazing (pun intended). It really is amazing grace, how sweet the sound, that saved a wretch like me.

The work is done. "It is finished," as Christ said (John 19:30). All that condemnation was finished the day he hung on that cross some 2,000 years ago. So stop the condemnation. You are free. If you've accepted it, it's yours.

Now, I could go on and on about grace. People write entire books on it. So if you are still having a hard time believing it, then do some digging. Look up all the references to it in Scripture. Read a good book on the subject. But most importantly, do all you can to believe it. As impossible as it seems, you can get beyond what you've done.

"NO GRACE FOR YOU!"

Now that I've completed my mini-sermon on grace, there is one more thing I need to get off my chest, and it's about the misconception that grace is something cheap. That is, that you can get it today and then go out and get back to the "fun" stuff, all the while planning on asking for forgiveness all over again once you've sown your wild oats. Grace isn't something that can be played around with. It isn't to be taken lightly. After all, it came at a very great price. So if you think that you can accept it while all along planning on going back into the same sinful situation again, think again. God knows your heart, remember? Like S. Claus, he knows if you've been bad or good, but he also knows if you are planning any more of the bad for sometime in the future. That kind of manipulation doesn't warrant God's grace. What I mean is that **if you think, "Oh, it's okay to keep on fooling around because 'God will always forgive me,'" you are wrong.** That's taking advantage. And he knows it. It's essentially lying—lying to God that you agree with him about how wrong it is to do what you did. If you are banking on God's forgiveness while deliberately going against his Word, then beware. He can't be fooled.

> The man who says, "I know him," but does not do what he commands is a liar, and the truth is not in him.
>
> 1 John 2:4

> No one who is born of God will continue to sin, because God's seed remains in him; he cannot go on sinning, because he has been born of God.
>
> 1 John 3:9

This verse used to give me fits. How can this be? I mean, no one keeps *all* his commands. We all continue to sin. And then I figured it out. This is the person who keeps on sinning, banking on the gift of grace. The person who says, "Oh, I'll just do this or that, because I can always ask for forgiveness later." Oops! Not according to 1 John 3:9. Now, that doesn't mean that you'll never mess up again. It only means that you won't go on living in sin as if it's acceptable practice to you because you are counting on his forgiveness. In the words of the Soup Nazi (if he were handing out grace in those bowls), "No grace for you!"

> If we claim to have fellowship with him yet walk in the darkness, we lie and do not live by the truth.
>
> 1 John 1:6

Don't become a liar. Once you choose God, you can't choose darkness. The two don't mesh. No taking grace for granted. This is why repentance is so essential. Sure, you might mess up again. In fact, you'll probably mess up again in some area of your life or another, but don't go into the mess-up thinking that it's okay because God will forgive you. That's not how it works. It takes a broken spirit and a contrite heart to really get to God's grace. You have to mean it when you say, "What I did was wrong."

But here's the amazing thing about how grace works. When going after God's forgiveness, you don't have to ask for it. It's already yours once you've confessed and agreed with God that what you did was wrong. So tell him what you did. Agree that it was stupid, wrong, bad, all that stuff, and then thank him. Thank him for the amazing gifts of forgiveness and grace.

DOING THE GRACE/REPENTANCE TWO-STEP

So let's review this simple two-step plan to get the kind of forgiveness we have been talking about here. It's all part of God's plan, and here is the rundown of the steps you can take to partake of the grace of God:

1. **Fess up. You did it.** You know what you did, and you know it's against God's Word. So get real. Get honest and tell yourself and God that what you did was wrong. 'Cuz if you don't, then you are a liar—not my words, God's. Scripture also tells us to confess our sins to another person. Be careful with this one. Don't just tell anyone—make sure they can be trusted. A pastor or trusted friend is your best choice. Having to tell someone what you did can be very embarrassing, and maybe the next time you are tempted to do something wrong you might remember how awful it is to have to confess it. So check out these passages from God's Word:

> If we say that we have no sin, we are deceiving ourselves and the truth is not in us. If we confess our sins, He is faithful and righteous to forgive us our sins and to cleanse us from all unrighteousness. If we say that we have not sinned, we make Him a liar and His word is not in us.
>
> 1 John 1:8–10 NASB

> Therefore confess your sins to each other and pray for each other so that you may be healed. The prayer of a righteous man is powerful and effective.
>
> James 5:16

2. **Change your ways.** The first and hardest step is to admit what you did wrong. But things don't get much easier from there. The next step is to change the way you do things. Stop doing what you did. Give it up. Get over it. It's called repentance. And without it, that confession you just made doesn't mean a thing. So here's the deal on repenting:

Repent = 1 : to turn from sin and dedicate oneself
to the amendment of one's life
2 a : to feel regret or contrition
b : to change one's mind[16]

And here's what God's Word has to say about it:

Repent, then, and turn to God, so that your sins may be wiped out, that times of refreshing may come from the Lord.

Acts 3:19

Set your minds on things above, not on earthly things.

Colossians 3:2

Therefore, if anyone is in Christ, he is a new creation; the old has gone, the new has come!

2 Corinthians 5:17

This all means you just need to realize that what's over is over. Remember, repentance is not only changing your life so it doesn't happen again, repentance also means "to change one's mind." You've moved on. Don't hang on to the past; you are a new creation. Stop worrying about what you did, and turn your mind upward. It's okay to feel "regret" in repentance. Just give up that old life and move forward to a new one.

NO PAIN, NO GAIN

Now, you might have done it all just right. You confessed, you repented, and you changed your life, but the pain is still there. Don't be alarmed. Don't think you've done something wrong or wonder why God hasn't taken away the agony. He can't, or rather won't, do that. His law is good, and it is there for a reason: to protect you. Even from yourself. The things that God forbids can and most often **do** hurt you. That's why he forbids them—for your own protection. And just having confessed and turned from a behavior doesn't take away the effects of your actions. What you did has consequences; side effects, if you will. And research seems to show that these side effects are being felt by many a teenager across the world. Sex doesn't go unpunished. It's not something we do that leaves us unaffected. Sex of any kind affects us spiritually, emotionally, mentally, and physically (more on that in "Sexual Activity Leads to Depression," page 99). So what you think about sex and how you treat it is of utmost importance in your life today. Forgiveness and grace won't take away the pain, but they will give you hope and a fresh start. So don't shake your fist at God if he seems to be silent while you suffer from heartache, disease, or unwanted pregnancy. It's part of the results of your actions. But rest in the knowledge that he does work all things together for the good of those who love him (Romans 8:28) and that he truly, truly loves the repentant soul.

TO BREAK UP OR NOT TO BREAK UP

To break up or not to break up, that is the question. You've confessed your mess. You've gotten forgiveness and you want to move on, so what do you do about the guy? If you are in a relationship with him, does it mean you break it all off? Burn all your bridges? Get while the getting's good? Not necessarily. That might be your first instinct. It might be the advice you've gotten from trusted friends (and good advice at that), but before you make up your mind, just consider this.

I'm not interested in making the decision for you. I don't know your individual situation. But it's important to realize that once you've gone the distance, any distance, physically, it's easier and easier to keep going that far and farther in subsequent relationships. So you might run from this guy as fast as you can and think, "Phew! Glad I'm free from that temptation." But the truth is that the next guy who excites you will be just as much of a temptation. Usually it isn't about the guy but about you and your commitment to God's law. So if it makes sense to you and your situation, you might want to consider talking it out with your guy. If he agrees that you've gone too far, then you can help one another stay pure. You can set rules—places you won't go together or be alone together. You can enlist the help of friends, family, pastors, whoever, to help you keep your commitment to God's law. This could be an important step in learning not to run from mistakes in your relationships but to manage them, to repair them. In marriage, if you make a mistake, you can't run from each other; you have to work it out. And dating is the training ground for marriage. Now, I'm not saying categorically, "Stay with him." Don't get me wrong. It depends on the individual situation. Some relationships might be really destructive. For example, if he is a nonbeliever, then you **have** to get out. Or if he doesn't agree with your newfound faith in God's law, then no amount of precaution-taking will help you keep your promises to God. So be smart about it. Consider the guy, your God, and yourself, and make a wise decision. One that will best ensure that you will keep your body to yourself.

If through a broken heart God can bring His purposes to pass in the world, then thank Him for breaking your heart.
Oswald Chambers

THE END OR JUST THE BEGINNING?

I'm sure I've said it enough already, but as a kind of period on the end of this "beyond technical" sentence, trust that there is hope for your heart. **You can change the way you are living.** You can get back to the foot of God. You can start fresh. And you can feel whole again. It probably won't happen in an instant, but then again, I never want to underestimate the power of a repentant heart in the hands of an all-powerful God. All I know for sure is that you can become clean. You can find a fresh start, and you can go on to have a wonderful life with the perfect guy. You can have a life that is holy and acceptable and a blast, all at the same time. So spend time in God's Word. Carry it with you. Engrave it on your heart, and hope against all hope that the best is yet to come in your life.

> So we fix our eyes not on what is seen, but on what is unseen. For what is seen is temporary, but what is unseen is eternal.
>
> 2 Corinthians 4:18

chapter 9

SO HOW FAR
Is Too Far?

I hope you didn't skip to the end of the book to read this chapter, because the entire book was meant to answer this question. This is just the conclusion. The wrap-up. The end of my tirade on sexuality and you. If you've read up to here, then hopefully you've already formed some kind of an opinion for yourself on how far is too far sexually. What you need to think about now is how you are going to handle yourself. How will you live according to your plans? How will you keep from crossing your line in the sand? A lot of ideas are floating around out there about how to stay pure. There are pledges you sign, jewelry you wear, and commitments you make, and they all are beneficial if, and only if, you have truly decided that you are committed to this new choice. **You have to make a conscious decision to change the way you think about sex.** You can't walk to the altar to make a pledge just because everyone else is doing it. And you can't do it because you wanna just give it a shot. You have to truly make a commitment to yourself—a commitment that saving yourself for marriage really means *saving* yourself. It means giving yourself the best chance at an amazing life.

Once you understand how guys can use your sexual activity and rip you off, you are a huge step closer to stepping away from the stuff you've been doing or thinking about doing and a lot closer to staying pure. Don't think of it just as a call to purity; think of it as a step in the right direction for your image, for your PR campaign, and for finding the perfect man. **Giving yourself away to any guy who is willing to take you is just putting the perfect guy farther and farther from your grasp.** Guys will lie to you to get what they want—and what they want is your sex—and then they are gone. So any guy who will fool around with you will use you up and then dump you. Sound like fun? Don't be a dummy. Don't lie to yourself and say, "This guy is different," because they are all the same. **If he will fool around with you, he will fool around with another girl and another.** You aren't that special; you are just someone who is willing. So don't be willing anymore to be duped by the guy plot to get a little free sex play.

Figure out who you want to be, what you want to project, and what kind of guy you ultimately want to catch, and then develop your plan for getting there. I promise you that every guy I played hard to get with—that is, every guy I didn't let have me—wanted to marry me. But every guy I pursued and chased and tried to lure into loving me ran away from me as fast as he could. Guys love a chase, and they love the elusive girl. So make the decision: do you want to be the easy and then "what the heck is she good for now" girl, or would you rather be the diamond everyone is hoping to get ahold of because you are so rare? The girl who won't fool around is rare, and that makes you alluring to guys. It makes you different, mysterious. No matter how much they beg and plead, they like you more when you say no. I knew one guy who would beg and plead with his dates to stay the night with him—no sex or anything, just stay the night. He said that if a girl did stay the night, then he instantly knew what kind of girl she was and he wouldn't see her again, but if she said no to all his urgings, then she might just be the girl for him. Pass the test—say no. It will make you much more alluring to him, I promise.

If you think you've gone too far and now you are feeling guilty, stop. As a believer you are no longer counted guilty by God because of his forgiveness. This forgiveness, based on your relationship with Christ, means you are no longer condemned. What you are feeling is simply conviction. You have gone down the wrong path, and your conscience is now tapping on your shoulder. You simply need to tell him what you've done. I know, he knows all, but you still have to tell him. It's called confession. Then you have to trust that he has forgiven you. And you have to repent—that is, turn away from your old behavior and move toward new behavior. I hope this is your plan. Because if you keep doing what you're doing, you'll keep getting what you've got. And my question is, is that enough? Or are you ready to move on to something more?

If you've kept yourself pure and you are now more determined than ever to continue down that path, keep it up! You can do it. Girls are more alluring to guys when they are pure. It's odd but

Wasting time
deploring the
past keeps God
at a distance.
Brennan Manning

true. Guys want what they can't get. So don't be fooled by any fancy lines or lies of the enemy. **Staying pure is the best way to eventually land the man of your dreams.** I promise, he's out there somewhere, and he's well worth the wait.

So **decide today how far is too far.** Consider all that you've read and all that God has written on the subject. Who do you want to be? How do you want to be thought of? Take a stand. Hold firm and stay strong through the hard times. You can do it, and you can be victorious.

DRAWING THE LINE

Just like in my book *Sexy Girls* where I had you draw the line of what kind of clothes you were going to wear, you're going to **draw the line sexually right here.** See, if there is no line, then it becomes a lot harder to stop when you're with the guy of your dreams. So before you put this book away, let's do some line drawing. Below is a list of stuff that you might one day want to do with a guy. They are kind of in a progression, from least sexual to most sexual—which is generally the path we take when it comes to getting physical. Have a look.

The Double Take (this is when you oogle your guy and can't stop)

Talking with him

Flirting with him

Touching his arm or leg

Holding hands

Touching each other's faces

Arms around each other

Kissing

Touching below the neck

Etc., etc. (I'm not going any farther because I think there's plenty of space above to start drawing your line)

So have a ponder. Where will you draw the line when it comes to guys? How far is too far for you? How far is too far for God? Draw a line under the most that you want to do with a guy before you are married.

Did you do it?

Good. Now you have something to work with. The next step in keeping it pure is to **talk to someone about your commitment.** Maybe a youth pastor, or parent, or even a really good friend, anyone who will help hold you accountable. Their job is to ask you, "Did you cross the line?" Remember, every time you have a date or spend time with a guy, your accountability partner is going to ask you how far you went. This will really help you when you're with the guy, because telling your confidant that you crossed the line is really sickening.

Also, if you haven't read *Dateable*, you might find some really good ideas in there about keeping the line you've drawn. It really helps to learn about the opposite sex and how much they appreciate the line being drawn, even if they act like they don't. The good guys will think more of a girl who has made up her mind to keep it clean, shall we say. Talk to him about the line you've drawn, so you can be on the same page. That way, if he's not a "good guy," he can get away while the getting's good instead of "working on you" to see if he can break your promise to yourself.

Here are some other things and places to avoid if you want to try to keep your line drawn right where it is:

No spending time in your room with him with the door closed.

No napping together.

No lying down together, period.

No hanging out at home alone.

No parking to "enjoy the view" or to "just talk."

No back rubs.

No drinking. (You can lose all memory of lines when you do.)

No dating nonbelievers. (They won't have respect for your lines.)

These are just a few situations that can make keeping your line where you've drawn it difficult. So they're things to avoid. Having a plan before you get into a relationship will help you handle that relationship in the way you have planned. And writing down that plan helps reinforce it in your mind and heart. So now I want you to write it down. Write a small prayer here, including your line and even some of the "no, no's" above. Make it a promise to God. Then, after you've written it, read it out loud to him and sign your name. This is your commitment. Your word. And your word shouldn't be broken. Ask God to help you keep your commitment and remember him every time you get into a sticky situation.

Dear God,

Signed _____

Well, this is it. It's good-bye for now. Hope you found some good stuff in this book. And I pray that your heart is strengthened and ready for the battle ahead. I am proud of you for coming this far. Keep the faith. I'm thinking about you.

Hayley

Your SPIRITUAL Entourage

Because God's Got Your Back

CONFESSING YOUR STUFF

If we confess our sins, he is faithful and just and will forgive us our sins and purify us from all unrighteousness.

1 John 1:9

I have sinned greatly in what I have done. Now, O LORD, I beg you, take away the guilt of your servant. I have done a very foolish thing.

2 Samuel 24:10

Therefore confess your sins to each other and pray for each other so that you may be healed. The prayer of a righteous man is powerful and effective.

James 5:16

He who conceals his sins does not prosper, but whoever confesses and renounces them finds mercy.

Proverbs 28:13

When I kept silent, my bones wasted away through my groaning all day long. For day and night your hand was heavy upon me; my strength was sapped as in the heat of summer. Then I acknowledged my sin to you and did not cover up my iniquity. I said, "I will confess my transgressions to the LORD"—and you forgave the guilt of my sin.

Psalm 32:3–5

FAILURE

We know that the law is spiritual; but I am unspiritual, sold as a slave to sin. . . . Therefore, there is now no condemnation for those who are in Christ Jesus.

Romans 7:14; 8:1

The LORD works out everything for his own ends—even the wicked for a day of disaster.

Proverbs 16:4

And we know that in all things God works for the good of those who love him, who have been called according to his purpose.

Romans 8:28

GETTING BACK TO GOD

Delight yourself in the LORD and he will give you the desires of your heart.

Psalm 37:4

Therefore we do not lose heart. Though outwardly we are wasting away, yet inwardly we are being renewed day by day.

2 Corinthians 4:16

Now faith is being sure of what we hope for and certain of what we do not see.

Hebrews 11:1

He replied, "Because you have so little faith. I tell you the truth, if you have faith as small as a mustard seed, you can say to this mountain, 'Move from here to there' and it will move. Nothing will be impossible for you."

Matthew 17:20

But when he asks, he must believe and not doubt, because he who doubts is like a wave of the sea, blown and tossed by the wind. That man should not think he will receive anything from the Lord.

James 1:6–7

STRENGTH FOR TODAY

Therefore put on the full armor of God, so that when the day of evil comes, you may be able to stand your ground, and after you have done everything, to stand. Stand firm then, with the belt of truth buckled around your waist, with the breastplate of righteousness in place, and with your feet fitted with the readiness that comes from the gospel of peace. In addition to all this, take up the shield of faith, with which you can extinguish all the flaming arrows of the evil one. Take the helmet of salvation and the sword of the Spirit, which is the word of God.

Ephesians 6:13–17

My son, if you accept my words and store up my commands within you, turning your ear to wisdom and applying your heart to understanding, and if you call out for insight and cry aloud for understanding, and if you look for it as for silver and search for it as for hidden treasure, then you will understand the fear of the LORD and find the knowledge of God.

Proverbs 2:1–5

So do not fear, for I am with you; do not be dismayed, for I am your God. I will strengthen you and help you; I will uphold you with my righteous right hand.

Isaiah 41:10

In you, O LORD, I have taken refuge; let me never be put to shame; deliver me in your righteousness. Turn your ear to me, come quickly to my rescue; be my rock of refuge, a strong fortress to save me.

Psalm 31:1–2

What, then, shall we say in response to this? If God is for us, who can be against us? He who did not spare his own Son, but gave him up for us all—how will he not also, along with him, graciously give us all things? Who will bring any charge against those whom God has chosen? It is God who justifies.

Romans 8:31–33

The reason the Son of God appeared was to destroy the devil's work.

1 John 3:8

But Jesus immediately said to them: "Take courage! It is I. Don't be afraid."

Matthew 14:27

God is our refuge and strength, an ever-present help in trouble.

Psalm 46:1

FEELING TEMPTATION

Be always on the watch, and pray that you may be able to escape all that is about to happen, and that you may be able to stand before the Son of Man.

Luke 21:36

For our struggle is not against flesh and blood, but against the rulers, against the authorities, against the powers of this dark world and against the spiritual forces of evil in the heavenly realms.

Ephesians 6:12

In the same way, the Spirit helps us in our weakness. We do not know what we ought to pray for, but the Spirit himself intercedes for us with groans that words cannot express.

Romans 8:26

Like a city whose walls are broken down is a man who lacks self-control.

Proverbs 25:28

BREAKING UP

Am I now trying to win the approval of men, or of God? Or am I trying to please men? If I were still trying to please men, I would not be a servant of Christ.

Galatians 1:10

I remember my affliction and my wandering, the bitterness and the gall. I well remember them, and my soul is downcast within me. Yet this I call to mind and therefore I have hope: Because of the LORD's great love we are not consumed, for his compassions never fail. They are new every morning; great is your faithfulness. I say to myself, "The LORD is my portion; therefore I will wait for him."

Lamentations 3:19–24

It is to a man's honor to avoid strife, but every fool is quick to quarrel.

Proverbs 20:3

Trust in the LORD with all your heart and lean not on your own understanding; in all your ways acknowledge him, and he will make your paths straight.

Proverbs 3:5–6

Each one should test his own actions. Then he can take pride in himself, without comparing himself to somebody else, for each one should carry his own load.

Galatians 6:4–5

The suffering won't last forever. It won't be long before this generous God who has great plans for us in Christ—eternal and glorious plans they are!—will have you put together and on your feet for good.

1 Peter 5:10 Message

PRE-DATE PREPARATION

Do not conform any longer to the pattern of this world, but be transformed by the renewing of your mind. Then you will be able to test and approve what God's will is—his good, pleasing and perfect will.

Romans 12:2

The end of all things is near. Therefore be clear minded and self-controlled so that you can pray.

1 Peter 4:7

Create in me a pure heart, O God, and renew a steadfast spirit within me. Do not cast me from your presence or take your Holy Spirit from me. Restore to me the joy of your salvation and grant me a willing spirit, to sustain me. Then I will teach transgressors your ways, and sinners will turn back to you. Save me from bloodguilt, O God, the God who saves me, and my tongue will sing of your righteousness. O Lord, open my lips, and my mouth will declare your praise.

Psalm 51:10–15

"Not by might nor by power, but by My Spirit," says the LORD of hosts.

Zechariah 4:6 NASB

Those who belong to Christ Jesus have crucified the sinful nature with its passions and desires.

Galatians 5:24

Then Jesus said to his disciples, "If anyone would come after me, he must deny himself and take up his cross and follow me."

Matthew 16:24

Flee immorality. Every other sin that a man commits is outside the body, but the immoral man sins against his own body.

1 Corinthians 6:18 NASB

But immorality or any impurity or greed must not even be named among you, as is proper among saints.

Ephesians 5:3 NASB

For this is the will of God, your sanctification; that is, that you abstain from sexual immorality.

1 Thessalonians 4:3 NASB

Now the deeds of the flesh are evident, which are: immorality, impurity, sensuality.

Galatians 5:19 NASB

FRIENDS MAKING FUN OF YOU

Consider it pure joy, my brothers, whenever you face trials of many kinds.

James 1:2

But I say to you, love your enemies and pray for those who persecute you.

Matthew 5:44 NASB

Never pay back evil for evil to anyone. Respect what is right in the sight of all men.

Romans 12:17 NASB

For I consider that the sufferings of this present time are not worthy to be compared with the glory that is to be revealed to us.

Romans 8:18 NASB

WANTING GOD'S FORGIVENESS

In Him we have redemption through His blood, the forgiveness of our trespasses, according to the riches of His grace.

Ephesians 1:7 NASB

Therefore let it be known to you, brethren, that through Him forgiveness of sins is proclaimed to you.

Acts 13:38 NASB

Therefore there is now no condemnation for those who are in Christ Jesus.

Romans 8:1 NASB

If you confess with your mouth Jesus as Lord, and believe in your heart that God raised Him from the dead, you will be saved.

Romans 10:9 NASB

He Himself bore our sins in His body on the cross, so that we might die to sin and live to righteousness; for by His wounds you were healed.

1 Peter 2:24 NASB

When you were dead in your transgressions and the uncircumcision of your flesh, He made you alive together with Him, having forgiven us all our transgressions.

Colossians 2:13 NASB

FORGIVING THE GUY

If you forgive men when they sin against you, your heavenly Father will also forgive you.

Matthew 6:14

My heavenly Father will also do the same to you, if each of you does not forgive his brother from your heart.

Matthew 18:35 NASB

Whenever you stand praying, forgive, if you have anything against anyone, so that your Father who is in heaven will also forgive you your transgressions.

Mark 11:25 NASB

FEELING GUILTY

By grace you have been saved through faith; and that not of yourselves, it is the gift of God.

Ephesians 2:8 NASB

Let us then approach the throne of grace with confidence, so
that we may receive mercy and find grace to help us in our time
of need.

Hebrews 4:16

For what I am doing, I do not understand; for I am not practicing
what I would like to do, but I am doing the very thing I hate. But
if I do the very thing I do not want to do, I agree with the Law,
confessing that the Law is good. So now, no longer am I the one
doing it, but sin which dwells in me.

Romans 7:15–17 NASB

FIGHTING THE MEMORY

Do not be anxious about anything, but in everything, by prayer and petition, with thanksgiving, present your requests to God. And the peace of God, which transcends all understanding, will guard your hearts and your minds in Christ Jesus. Finally, brothers, whatever is true, whatever is noble, whatever is right, whatever is pure, whatever is lovely, whatever is admirable—if anything is excellent or praiseworthy—think about such things.

Philippians 4:6–8

I consider that our present sufferings are not worth comparing with the glory that will be revealed in us.

Romans 8:18

And the God of all grace, who called you to his eternal glory in Christ, after you have suffered a little while, will himself restore you and make you strong, firm and steadfast.

1 Peter 5:10

1. Third annual Teen Sex Survey in the October 2005 issue of *Teen People* magazine.

2. *Teen People*, Sept. 2, 2005.

3. http://www.teenpregnancy.org/resources/teens/avoid/abstinence/absfacts.asp, National Campaign to Prevent Teen Pregnancy. (2003). *With one voice: America's adults and teens sound off about teen pregnancy.* Washington, DC.

4. C. Birnbaum, The love & sex survey 2000, *Twist*, Oct./Nov. 2000, 54–56.

5. News release, *Seventeen* News: National survey conducted by *Seventeen* finds that more than half of teens ages 15–19 have engaged in oral sex, Feb. 28, 2000.

6. Meg Meeker, M.D., *Epidemic: How Teen Sex Is Killing Our Kids* (Washington, D.C.: LifeLine Press, 2002), 16.

7. Megan Rauscher, "Oral Human Papillomavirus (HPV) Is Tied to Sexual Behavior and HIV Status," HIVandHepatitus.com, March 10, 2004, http://www.hivandhepatitis.com/recent/ois/humanpapillomavirus/031004l.html.

8. Center for Disease Control Trends in Reportable STDs "General Research" in U.S. 2003.

9. US Bureau of Statistics

10. Kara Joyner and J. Richard Udry, "You Don't Bring Me Anything But Down: Adolescent Romance and Depression," *Journal of Health and Social Behavior* 41 (2000): 369–91.

11. Armand M. Nocholi Jr., M.D., ed., *The Harvard Guide to Psychiatry,* 3rd ed. (Cambridge, MA: Belknap Press, 1999), 622–23.

12. A. M. Culp, M. M. Clyman, and R. E. Culp, "Adolescent Depressed Mood, Reports of Suicide Attempts, and Asking for Help," *Adolescence* 30 (1995): 827–37.

13. National Longitudinal Survey of Adolescent Health, Wave II, 1996.

14. Meeker, *Epidemic*, 63.

15. Walter A. Elwell and Philip Wesley Comfort, *Tyndale Bible Dictionary,* Tyndale Reference Library (Wheaton: Tyndale, 2001), 550.

16. *Merriam-Webster's Collegiate Dictionary*, 10th ed., s.v. "Repent."

Hayley DiMarco writes cutting-edge and best-selling books including *Mean Girls: Facing Your Beauty Turned Beast*, *Marriable: Taking the Desperate Out of Dating*, *Dateable: Are You? Are They?*, *The Dateable Rules*, and *The Dirt on Breaking Up*. Her goal is to give practical answers for life's problems and encourage girls to form stronger spiritual lives. From traveling the world with a French theater troupe to working for a little shoe company called Nike, Hayley has seen a lot of life and decided to make a difference in her world. Hayley is Chief Creative Officer and founder of Hungry Planet, an independent publishing imprint and communications company that feeds the world's appetite for truth. Hungry Planet helps organizations understand and reach the multitasking mind-set, while Hungry Planet books tackle life's everyday issues with a distinctly modern spiritual voice.

To keep the conversation going log on to
www.howfaris2far.com.

And for more on Hayley's other books
check out
www.hungryplanet.net.

Ditch MEAN for good
with help from Hayley!

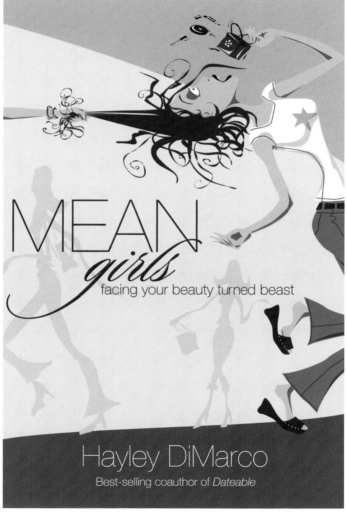

MEAN *girls*

facing your beauty turned beast

Hayley DiMarco

Best-selling coauthor of *Dateable*

Available at your local bookstore

If what you're showing ain't on the menu, keep it covered up!

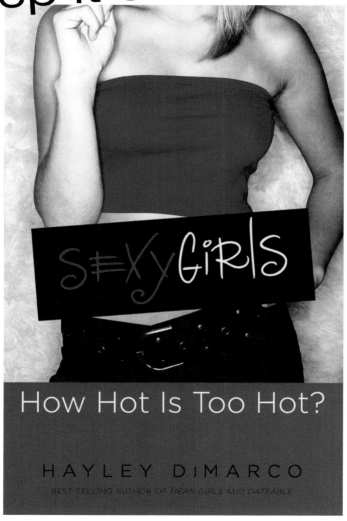

SEXY GIRLS

How Hot Is Too Hot?

HAYLEY DiMARCO

BEST SELLING AUTHOR OF *MEAN GIRLS* AND *DATEABLE*

Available at your local bookstore

"Feeding the World's Appetite for Truth"

What makes Hungry Planet books different?

Every Hungry Planet book attacks the senses of the reader with a postmodern mind-set (both visually and mentally) in a way unlike most books in the marketplace. Attention to every detail from physical appearance (book size, titling, cover, and interior design) to message (content and author's voice) helps Hungry Planet books connect with the more "visual" reader in ways that ordinary books can't.

With writing and packaging content for the young adult and "hip adult" markets, Hungry Planet books combine cutting-edge design with felt-need topics, all the while injecting a much-needed spiritual voice.

Why are publishers so eager to work with Hungry Planet?

Because of the innovative success and profitable track record of HP projects from the best-selling *Dateable* and *Mean Girls* to the Gold Medallion-nominated *The Dirt on Sex* (part of HP's The Dirt series). Publishers also take notice of HP founder Hayley (Morgan) DiMarco's past success in creating big ideas like the "Biblezine" concept while she was brand manager for Thomas Nelson Publishers' teen book division.

How does Hungry Planet come up with such big ideas?

Hayley and HP general manager/husband Michael DiMarco tend to create their best ideas at mealtime, which in the DiMarco household is around five times a day. Once the big idea and scope of the topic are established, the couple decides either to write the content themselves or find an up-and-coming author with a passion for the topic. HP then partners with a publisher to create the book.

How do I find out more about Hungry Planet?

Use the Web, silly—www.hungryplanet.net